Dinosaur Hunters in the Forest

Thanks to the creative team:
Senior Editor: Alice Peebles
Consultant: Neil Clark
Design: Perfect Bound Ltd

Hungry Tomato®
A division of Lerner Publishing Group, Inc.
241 First Avenue North
Minneapolis, MN 55401 USA

For reading levels and more information, look up
this title at www.lernerbooks.com.

Main body text set in Graviola Soft 12/14.

Library of Congress Cataloging-in-Publication Data

Names: Mason, Paul, 1967– author. | Leonard, Andre, 1954– author.
Title: Dinosaur hunters in the forest / Paul Mason, Andre Leonard.
Description: Minneapolis : Hungry Tomato, [2018] | Series: Dinosaurs rule |
Audience: Ages 8–12. | Audience: Grades 4 to 6. | Includes index. | Identifiers:
LCCN 2017057010 (print) | LCCN 2017061820 (ebook) | ISBN 9781541524002
(eb pdf) | ISBN 9781541501041 (lb : alk. paper)
Subjects: LCSH: Dinosaurs—Juvenile literature. | Dinosaurs—Behavior—
Juvenile literature.
Classification: LCC QE861.5 (ebook) | LCC QE861.5 M34297 2018 (print) | DDC
567.9—dc23

LC record available at https://lccn.loc.gov/2017057010

Manufactured in the United States of America
1-43775-33633-4/16/2018

Dinosaur Hunters in the Forest

by Paul Mason

Illustrated by Andre Leonard

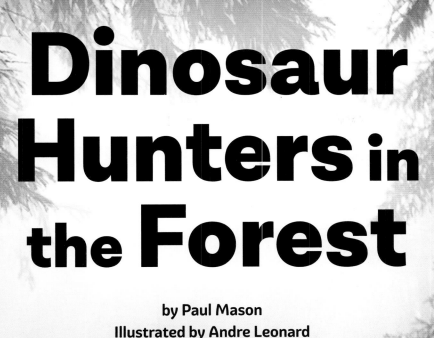

HUNGRY TOMATO™

MINNEAPOLIS

Contents

Planet Dinosaur

Dinosaurs lived on Earth for more than 160 million years. There were dinosaurs of all shapes and sizes, and they lived in many different places.

One place where dinosaurs lived was forests. The trees and ferns provided predators with places to lie in ambush. Smaller, faster dinosaurs could zip through the undergrowth to escape.

Triassic world
(250–201 million years ago)

The first dinosaurs appeared during the Triassic Period, when a giant land mass called Pangaea was the main land on Earth. It was hot and dry. Forests of tall conifer trees and ferns grew mainly near rivers.

Jurassic world
(201–145 million years ago)

Next came the Jurassic Period. Pangaea broke up, forming new land masses. Mountains appeared and rain became more common. With more rain, the number of rivers and forested areas grew.

Cretaceous world
(145–66 million years ago)

The final age of the dinosaurs was the Cretaceous Period. Earth's land masses continued to break up and form the continents we know today. More forests grew. This was a top time to be a dinosaur if you were a hunter in the forest.

A Tasty Find
Quetzalcoatlus vs. Alamosaurus

These *Quetzalcoatlus* have made a lucky find: a young, dead *Alamosaurus*. It must have been killed by a big predator last night, then abandoned.

Fresh *Alamosaurus* meat makes a nice change for *Quetzalcoatlus*. It normally spends its time hunting for small reptiles and perhaps fish. Its long beak enables it to hunt in a similar way to a modern-day stork.

Alamosaurus

Alamosaurus lived long after most giant dinosaurs had disappeared from North America. With no rivals, *Alamosaurus* wandered through the open woodlands, using its long neck to feed on high-up vegetation almost undisturbed.

It just had to keep an eye out for predators—such as *Tyrannosaurus*.

Last titanosaur
Alamosaurus was one of the last titanosaurs—a group of giant-sized dinosaurs.

KILLER FACT

Alamosaurus was probably one of the biggest dinosaurs ever—almost the size of 115 foot (35 m) long *Argentinosaurus*, the record holder from Argentina.

Crossing over
Some experts think *Alamosaurus* migrated from South America via a land bridge that appeared 71 million years ago.

SCALE

FACT FILE

Alive: 72–66 million years ago
Order and Family: Saurischia/ Saltasauridae
Length: 98 ft. (30 m)
Height: 26 ft. (8 m)
Weight: 77 tons (70 t)
Diet: herbivorous
Fossils found: an almost-complete juvenile specimen from Texas, and many other fragments
Location: southwestern United States

Quetzalcoatlus

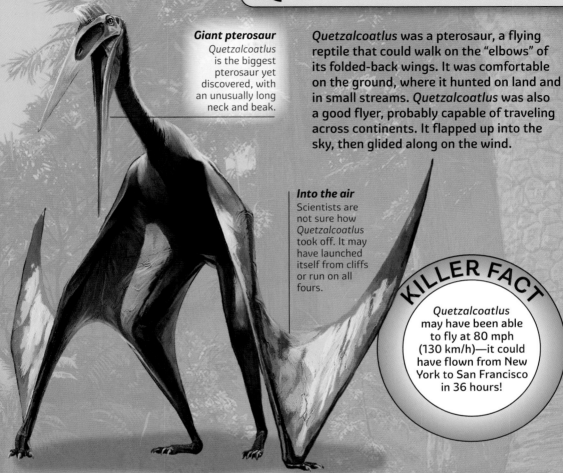

Giant pterosaur
Quetzalcoatlus is the biggest pterosaur yet discovered, with an unusually long neck and beak.

Quetzalcoatlus was a pterosaur, a flying reptile that could walk on the "elbows" of its folded-back wings. It was comfortable on the ground, where it hunted on land and in small streams. *Quetzalcoatlus* was also a good flyer, probably capable of traveling across continents. It flapped up into the sky, then glided along on the wind.

Into the air
Scientists are not sure how *Quetzalcoatlus* took off. It may have launched itself from cliffs or run on all fours.

KILLER FACT

Quetzalcoatlus may have been able to fly at 80 mph (130 km/h)—it could have flown from New York to San Francisco in 36 hours!

SCALE

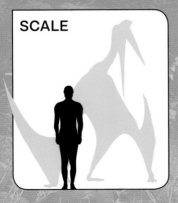

FACT FILE

Alive: 70–65 million years ago
Order and Family: Pterosauria/ Azhdarchidae
Length: 16 ft. (5 m)
Wingspan: 33–36 ft. (10–11 m)
Weight: 440 lb. (200 kg)
Diet: carnivorous
Fossils found: fragments only
Location: Texas

Snap Attack!
Sinornithosaurus vs. Sulcavis

Sinornithosaurus has spotted a meal—but it needs to be quick! Its potential dinner is *Sulcavis*, one of the birds that have started to appear in the dinosaur world.

Sulcavis is an excellent flyer. For *Sinornithosaurus* the only chance of a snack is to grab *Sulcavis* before it whizzes off.

Sinornithosaurus

Sinornithosaurus was a quick, agile hunter, able to chase prey on the forest floor. It may also have hunted by dropping down from the trees, like an owl dropping on a mouse. *Sinornithosaurus*'s curved claws could grip branches and prey, and the long sickle claw on each back foot sliced into victims.

24-hour hunter
In 2011, scientists discovered that *Sinornithosaurus*'s eyes would have enabled it to hunt by day or night.

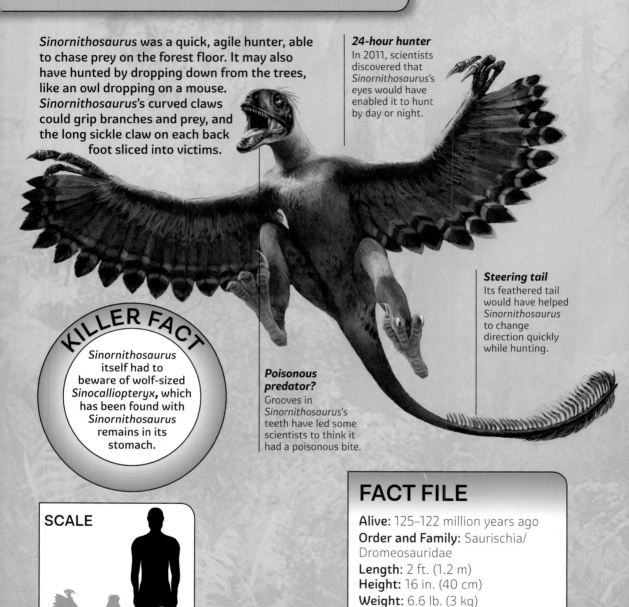

Steering tail
Its feathered tail would have helped *Sinornithosaurus* to change direction quickly while hunting.

KILLER FACT

Sinornithosaurus itself had to beware of wolf-sized *Sinocalliopteryx,* which has been found with *Sinornithosaurus* remains in its stomach.

Poisonous predator?
Grooves in *Sinornithosaurus*'s teeth have led some scientists to think it had a poisonous bite.

SCALE

FACT FILE

Alive: 125–122 million years ago
Order and Family: Saurischia/Dromeosauridae
Length: 2 ft. (1.2 m)
Height: 16 in. (40 cm)
Weight: 6.6 lb. (3 kg)
Diet: carnivorous
Fossils found: several almost-complete specimens
Location: northeast China

Sulcavis

Like many early birds, *Sulcavis* had teeth. (Even today some chickens still develop with teeth, though any that do will not survive.) What's more, *Sulcavis*'s teeth seem to have been quite specialized. They had strengthening ridges on the inside, which may show that *Sulcavis* ate hard-shelled prey such as snails or crabs.

Gripping claws
Like modern birds of prey, *Sulcavis* would have used its claws to grip onto prey.

Teeth for life
Just as most birds were evolving without teeth, *Sulcavis* was developing teeth to match its special diet.

KILLER FACT

Sulcavis gets its name from a combination of two Latin words. *Sulcus* means "groove" (for its grooved teeth), and *avis* means "bird."

FACT FILE

Alive: 125–121 million years ago
Family: Bohaiornithidae
Length: 6 in. (15 cm)
Wingspan: 8–10 in. (20–25 cm)
Weight: 0.7 oz. (20 g)
Diet: probably carnivorous, but possibly omnivorous
Fossils found: almost-complete fossils showing teeth and feathers
Location: northeast China

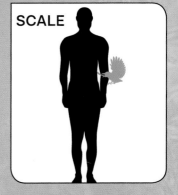

SCALE

Armor Defense
Saichania vs. Tarbosaurus

Saichania spends most of its time in drier landscapes but has come to the forested river valley to drink. This has turned out to be a mistake—lying in wait is a predatory tyrannosaur: *Tarbosaurus*.

Saichania is far from defenseless. Its armored body gives it protection, and one swipe of its powerful clubbed tail could badly injure *Tarbosaurus*.

Saichania

Saichania had a coat of natural armor that would have made it tricky to kill. Its head, chest, neck, back, and tail were covered in "osteoderms"—bony plates that provided protection. At the end of its tail was a club made of three osteoderms. This could be swung back and forth as Saichania ran off or used for whacking attackers if Saichania was cornered.

Neck defenses
Saichania's neck was completely protected by rings of bone, with the gaps between them covered by bony plates.

Stiffened tail
The last half of Saichania's tail was stiffened by rods under the skin, so it was a very effective weapon.

FACT FILE

Alive: 72–71 million years ago
Order and Family: Ornithischia/ Anklyosauridae
Length: 22 ft. (6.6 m)
Height: 8 ft. (2.4 m)
Weight: 2.2 tons (2 t)
Diet: herbivorous
Fossils found: complete and partial skulls and skeletons
Location: Mongolia

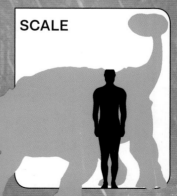

SCALE

Careful bite
Tarbosaurus could take huge bites when attacking but also carefully strip meat from bones.

Tarbosaurus

Tarbosaurus was one of the biggest tyrannosaurs. It was only a little smaller than its famous cousin from North America, *Tyrannosaurus rex*. *Tarbosaurus* actually had more teeth than *T. rex* but had weedier arms.

Experts think *Tarbosaurus* might have had a special bite that allowed it to tightly grip the large dinosaurs it usually hunted. These included *Saurolophus* and *Nemegtosaurus*.

KILLER FACT

In 1949, the remains of several *Tarbosaurus* were found together. Was this a family, or did the dinosaur ever hunt in packs? Scary! No one knows for sure.

Powerful legs
The back legs needed to be thick and powerful to support the heavy head and tail.

SCALE

FACT FILE

Alive: 72–68 million years ago
Family: Tyrannosauridae
Length: 31 ft. (9.5 m)
Height: 11 ft. (3.5 m)
Weight: 4.4 tons (4 t)
Diet: carnivorous
Fossils found: skulls and parts of several skeletons, adding up to every part of *Tarbosaurus*
Location: Mongolia and northern China

Forest Ambush
Eoraptor vs. Herrerasaurus

Two *Eoraptors* are feasting on a Panphagia they have killed—but this is a meal they will never finish. In fact, unless they watch out, it could be the last meal they ever eat!

Heading straight for them is their worst enemy: the bigger, stronger, and fiercer *Herrerasaurus*!

Eoraptor

With its slim build and long legs, *Eoraptor* was probably a fast runner. It was not a specialist hunter: *Eoraptor* ate whatever it could find. Its front teeth were long and sharp for cutting into meat, and its back teeth were flatter—more useful for grinding tough plants.

Omnivore
Eoraptor came from a time before most dinosaurs split between carnivores and herbivores. It ate both meat and plants.

Flexible neck
Its flexible neck helped *Eoraptor* if its prey suddenly tried to escape by changing direction.

KILLER FACT

Eoraptor was not actually a raptor. Raptors had long, curved sickle claws on their back feet— but *Eoraptor* did not.

Tearing claws
Eoraptor used its sharp claws to grip prey as it ripped it apart.

FACT FILE

Alive: 231–228 million years ago
Order: Saurischia
Length: 33 ft. (1 m)
Height: 28 in. (70 cm)
Weight: 22 lb. (10 kg)
Diet: omnivorous
Fossils found: two almost-complete skulls and skeletons
Location: northern Argentina

SCALE

Herrerasaurus

With its short thighs and long feet, *Herrerasaurus* was probably very fast. It was bigger than *Eoraptor*, though, and may have had trouble catching one in a race through the forest.

Herrerasaurus lived at a time when dinosaurs did not yet rule the earth. Its speed would have been useful for escaping non-dinosaur predators such as the fearsome, crocodile-like *Saurosuchus*.

Fossil dung
Fossilized dino dung (called *coprolites*) thought to be from *Herrerasaurus* shows it ate only meat and could digest bone.

Curved jaw
Herrerasaurus had a curve in its jaw, which scientists think helped it to grip struggling prey.

SCALE

FACT FILE

Alive: 231 million years ago
Order and Family: Saurischia/ Herrerasauridae
Length: 20 ft. (6 m)
Height: 5 ft. (1.6 m)
Weight: 772 lb. (350 kg)
Diet: carnivorous
Fossils found: two skulls and several parts of skeletons
Location: northern Argentina

High-Speed Pursuit

Afrovenator vs. Spinostropheus

Spinostropheus is a fast-moving dinosaur and can normally escape from attackers— but now it has a hungry *Afrovenator* on its tail. Despite being five times as heavy, *Afrovenator* can also move very quickly.

Spinostropheus needs to hit top speed as quickly as possible!

Afrovenator

Afrovenator was a "pursuit predator," like today's cheetahs and wolves. It was a lot bigger than either of them, though: *Afrovenator* weighed about a ton and must have made a lot of noise crashing through the forest chasing prey.

As one of the heavier dinosaurs, *Afrovenator* could not have stayed at top speed for long. If its victim escaped the first pursuit, it had a good chance of surviving.

Missing teeth
We can make a good guess at what its teeth were like—but actual teeth have been missing from Afrovenator remains.

KILLER FACT
Afrovenator had three claws on each hand and sharp teeth, all for ripping prey. It ran fast on its long back legs, and its stiff tail helped it to balance.

Longer arms
The arms were short but still longer than those of similar-looking dinosaurs.

SCALE

FACT FILE

Alive: 167–161 million years ago
Order and Family: Saurischia/ Megalosauridae
Length: 26 ft. (8 m)
Height: 8 ft. (2.3 m)
Weight: 1.1 tons (1 t)
Diet: carnivorous
Fossils found: most of a skull and parts of a skeleton
Location: west-central Africa (Niger)

Spinostropheus

Spinostropheus was a kind of Jurassic version of an ostrich (except it was a dinosaur, not a bird). It probably ate a mostly herbivorous diet, as well as insects and small animals.

The late Jurassic world had some heavyweight predators—the lightweight *Spinostropheus* could kick at attackers, but its main defense was a speedy escape.

Long-tailed
Spinostropheus used its long, flexible tail for balance, which made it easy to move around on two legs.

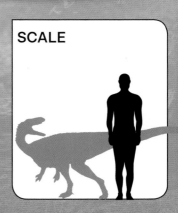

Long-legged
Long legs allowed *Spinostropheus* to run fast—useful when hunting and escaping larger predators.

FACT FILE

Alive: 167–161 million years ago
Order: Saurischia
Length: 13 ft. (4 m)
Height: 4 ft. 6 in. (1.4 m)
Weight: 440 lb. (200 kg)
Diet: omnivorous
Fossils found: part of a skeleton
Location: west-central Africa (Niger)

SCALE

Believe It or Not!

There were forests at the poles

During the Cretaceous Period, Earth was about 15°F hotter than today. It was so warm that forests were able to grow in the polar regions.

Dinosaur dung is very educational

Specimens of fossilized dinosaur dung, or coprolites, can tell scientists what dinosaurs ate, how healthy they were, and even whether they had parasites such as worms.

Trees can be fossils too

The remains of ancient trees can tell us a lot about the world of the dinosaurs, including what the climate was like in different places and how fast the trees grew.

Fossil trees killed a famous explorer—possibly

Famous explorer Robert Falcon Scott was one of the first people to find fossilized polar trees. The extra weight of the specimens he found (and tried to bring home) may be one reason why Scott did not make it back alive from his Antarctic expedition in 1912.

Some forest dinosaurs may have had night vision

Dinosaurs walked the forests of what is now the Antarctic—but how did they see during the long polar night? A fossilized *Leaellynasaura* may have the answer: unusually large parts of its brain were used for vision, which experts think would have helped it see in the dark.

Prehistoric trees are still around . . .

Scientists have discovered fossilized remains of ginkgo trees (also called maidenhair trees) that are 270 million years old. This tree grows in many places today. The monkey puzzle and Wollemia pine are also tree survivors from the age of dinosaurs.

Death of the Dinosaurs

Dinosaurs lived on Earth from 250 to 66 million years ago—and then, at the end of the Cretaceous Period, they disappeared. Many other animals and plants that were around at the time survived. It is difficult to be 100 percent sure what happened to kill off the dinosaurs but not these other living things. Here are the two main theories . . .

Volcanic eruptions

In India, a series of massive volcanic eruptions lasted for thousands of years. At first, the volcanoes spewed ash into the atmosphere, causing the temperature to drop.

The volcanoes also released poisonous gases, including greenhouse gases that rose up into the atmosphere and trapped heat. Over a long time, these gases caused such a rise in temperature that the sea became about 14°F hotter.

The dinosaurs could not cope with the changes that happened: sea levels rose, different plants and animals appeared, and the environment changed.

A huge meterorite hit the Earth

We now know that toward the end of the Age of Dinosaurs a huge meteorite, about 6 miles (10 km) across, hit Earth. It smashed down on Mexico's Yucatán Peninsula, causing forest fires, huge waves, and a cloud of dust that spread through the atmosphere.

The cloud from the meteorite impact, which made a huge, 110 mile (180 km) wide crater known as Chicxulub, blocked out sunlight around the world. The temperature dropped and the dinosaurs could not adapt.

Fall of the dinosaurs, rise of the mammals

What actually killed the dinosaurs is probably a combination of both events. First, climate change caused by volcanoes wiped out many dinosaurs. Then those that were left could not survive the aftereffects of the meteorite impact.

What did happen was that Earth was suddenly a lot less crowded without the dinosaurs roaming around. This made space for another kind of animal to become more successful: mammals. Eventually, the mammals we know best came to dominate . . .

Index

The Author

Paul Mason is a prolific author of children's books, many award-nominated, on such subjects as 101 ways to save the planet, vile things that go wrong with the human body, and the world's looniest inventors. Many contain surprising, unbelievable, or just plain revolting facts. Today, he lives at a secret location on the coast of Europe, where his writing shack usually smells of drying wetsuit (he's a former international swimmer and a keen surfer).

The Illustrator

Andre Leonard trained at Camberwell art school in London and at Leicester University. He has illustrated prolifically for leading magazines and book publishers, and his paintings are in a number of private collections worldwide. Andre prefers to work digitally but sometimes combines this with traditional media. He lives in Stamford, UK, with his wife, children, and a cat called Kimi, and he loves flying and sailing.

Glossary

carnivorous: living on a diet of meat. Carnivorous dinosaurs probably all hunted for food, though some may also have eaten already-dead animals.

family: label given to groups of dinosaurs that had similar physical characteristics but were not exactly alike

fossil: remains of a living thing from long ago. Fossils can be the remains of bones, shells, pieces of wood, plants—there are even fossilized footprints.

herbivorous: living on a diet of plants. Herbivorous dinosaurs would have been most plentiful wherever there was a good supply of plants and water.

order: one of two groups of dinosaurs that were divided based on the way their hips worked

omnivorous: living on a diet that combined meat and plants

Ornithischia: one of the two orders of dinosaur. Ornithischian dinosaurs were "bird-hipped," with hips that looked similar to a bird's.

Pterosauria: group of flying reptiles from the time of the dinosaurs, whose name means "winged lizard"

Saurischia: one of the two orders of dinosaur. Saurischian dinosaurs were "lizard-hipped," with hips that looked like a modern lizard's.

sickle: curved shape, with a pointed end. Some sickles also have a knife-like edge on their inside curve.

Picture credits